Unlock the full potential of Jimi Hendrix's iconic guitar tabs with the ultimate companion to this book. If you find yourself yearning for the exact location of a tab for any of the songs featured herein, look no further than our online store, where musical magic awaits. Visit us at

https://paidtabs.com/u/BlackBook,

and discover a treasure trove of musical mastery. Each song is meticulously crafted and available in PDF and GP formats that can be played on Guitar Pro. Immerse yourself in a more interactive and engaging experience as you explore the nuances of Hendrix's legendary tunes. Elevate your musical journey – dive into the soulful world of Jimi Hendrix with our premium tabs.

Table of Contents

How to read a tab

Understanding Tab

Guitar tab, or tablature, stands out as a widely embraced method for notating guitar music. Its allure lies in the ease of reading once you've grasped its intricacies.

To delve into tab comprehension, envision the guitar neck as though you're poised to play, gazing down upon it. Tab comprises six horizontal lines mirroring the guitar strings, with the thickest string aligning at the bottom and the thinnest at the top.

The essence of Tab
Upon these lines, numbers denote finger placements on the guitar fretboard. In decoding the diagram below, executing it on the guitar involves positioning your finger just behind the 2nd fret on the 5th string, followed by playing the note at the 4th fret, and then revisiting the 2nd fret. The 'zero' signifies playing an open string. In the language of musical notes, this sequence translates to B, C#, B, A.

Guitar Tab Chords

Tabbing a chord involves aligning the notes in a vertical line along the horizontal ones. Illustrated here is a C Chord. To properly interpret this tab, a single sweeping motion should be employed to strum the bottom 5 strings of the guitar.

```
e|--------0--
B|--------1--
G|--------0--
D|--------2--
A|--------3--
E|-----------
```

In this particular instance, the 'C Chord' is to be strummed thrice:

```
e|--0----0----0--
B|--1----1----1--
G|--0----0----0--
D|--2----2----2--
A|--3----3----3--
E|---------------
```

Hammer-On

Executing a hammer-on involves plucking a note and then forcefully pressing down with the fretting hand on the second note. Notably, the second note is not plucked but resonates as an echo of the first. In tab notation, hammer-ons are depicted as follows:

Pull-Off

Pull-offs, conversely, entail playing the first note again and then smoothly lifting the finger off with the fretting hand, allowing the one behind it to sound. The tab representation for pull-offs is structured as follows:

Bends

When the fretting hand induces a string to bend, producing a distinctive wobbling effect, it introduces what is known as a bend. This technique is commonly employed in solos and is tabbed in the following manner:

Release Bend

A release bend is akin to a standard bend, but it specifies the moment to ease off the bend and transition to the subsequent note.

Slide

As for a slide, the process commences with plucking the initial note and smoothly transitioning along the string either upward or downward to reach the second note. In the provided tab, the sequence involves playing the first note on the 10th fret and subsequently sliding the finger maintaining that note down to the 8th fret (a slide-down):

Legato Slide

In this context, the slide mirrors the conventional approach, with the distinction that the second note is not plucked, adhering to the typical slide technique.

In this scenario, a slide-up is executed by smoothly transitioning the finger from the 3rd fret to the 5th without lifting it:

Slight Left Hand Vibrato

Vibrato introduces a constant rhythmic modulation of the string. This entails a swift upward and downward bending, generating a dynamic, oscillating sound. Slight Left Hand Vibrato is depicted in tab notation as follows:

Wide Left Hand Vibrato

To achieve a more pronounced pitch variation, the fretting hand employs a wider vibrato, which is tabbed as:

Vibrato w/ Trem. Bar

Utilizing the tremolo bar constitutes another method for inducing vibrato. If a beat encompasses multiple notes, this effect is applied uniformly to all the chord's notes. The Wide vibrato, in comparison to the Slight one, imparts a more noticeable and expansive modulation.

Let ring

The "Let ring" directive instructs you to sustain the note until the conclusion of the dashed line. In tab notation, it appears as follows:

Palm Mute

Creating a palm mute effect involves using the side of your right hand (the fourth finger side) to lightly touch the string at the bridge's edge. This imparts a muted quality to the played notes.

Ghost Note

A ghost note is best described as a note that is felt but not heard distinctly. It is played softer, lacking emphasis, and can be executed by fretting a note without picking it. Ghost notes, symbolized by round brackets in notation, contribute subtly to the musical ambiance, adding nuance to the overall feel.

Dead Note

A dead note involves muting the strings using your left hand, achieved by lightly resting your left hand across the strings without applying pressure against the fret. The tab notation for a dead note appears as follows:

Up/Down Strokes

For a sequence of chords, the playing technique is specified with downstrokes, upstrokes, or a combination. In tab notation, the direction of strokes is denoted as follows:

Up/Down Arpeggios

When employing the arpeggio technique, chords are played with rapid succession, allowing the individual notes within the chord to be heard distinctly. Up/Down Arpeggios are tabbed as follows:

Natural Harmonics

Natural harmonics produce a bell-like resonance when a string is touched over a specific fret bar. The commonly used notation features the fret to be touched, preceded by a rhombus sign.

Polyphony

Polyphony, a musical texture comprising two or more independent lines of melody playing simultaneously, is represented in tabs. One of these lines is depicted in gray, indicating the fret number, while the other is shown in black.

Pinch Harmonic

A pinch harmonic, a guitar technique for creating artificial harmonics, involves the player's thumb or index finger on the picking hand slightly catching the string that was plucked. This action suppresses the fundamental frequency of the string, allowing one of the harmonics to take precedence.

Rhythm Notation

Tabs exclusively convey information about the pitch of notes and lack details about rhythm or note durations. Consequently, a tab can be played in various ways. While platforms like Songsterr provide the ability to visualize and audibly experience the tab as it's played, incorporating rhythm notation offers precise instructions on when to play a note and how long to sustain it. Rhythm notation closely resembles traditional sheet music notation (scores). Below, the fundamentals of rhythm notation are elucidated.

The Beat

Music is inherently bound by time, with a recurring pulse known as the beat forming the rhythmic foundation. This beat serves as a steady rhythm, inviting foot taps or dance moves. Visualize any music from a dance club, and the beat becomes immediately apparent—the constant element of time around which the music revolves.

Bars

To maintain structure in music, beats are organized into bars, also known as measures, each demarcated by bar lines. Typically, many songs comprise four beats per bar. The rhythmic cadence follows a sequential count: 4 ,3 ,2 ,1 ,4 ,3 ,2 ,1, and so forth, with beat one always signaling the onset of a new bar.

Time Signature

In tab notation, the time signature at the beginning of each tab serves as a guide. This fraction, with the top number representing the beats per bar (often 4), and the bottom number indicating the note value equivalent to each beat (usually 4), establishes the rhythmic framework. In essence, a time signature like 4/4 denotes that each bar encompasses four quarter notes, defining the pulse of the music.

Notes and Rests

Rhythm notation involves modifying the appearance of notes to signify their relative duration within a tab, while rests indicate the corresponding periods of silence. The nomenclature of notes and rests stems from their fractional value in relation to what constitutes a beat:

	NOTE	REST
Whole	(not signet)	▬
Half	╎	▬
Quater	╎	⌐
Eighth	╚	⅂
Sixteenth	╚	ⅎ
Thirty-Second	╚	ⅎ

Basic rhythmic values are essentially simple fractions of the 4-beat whole note. Consider the rhythm notation in the tab below:

In this illustration, each note carries the value of a quarter, lasting one beat each. The tempo at which you play the tab can vary, but the relative duration remains consistent (one note for one beat). Another instance:

D5

All rhythm values can be derived from combining two values, each half the duration of the other:

╎ + ╎ = ╎	▬ = ⌐ + ⌐
╚ + ╚ = ╎	⌐ = ⅂ + ⅂
╚ + ╚ = ╚	⅂ = ⅎ + ⅎ
╚ + ╚ = ╚	ⅎ = ⅎ + ⅎ

Here, a pause with a duration of half (equivalent to two beats) precedes the repetition of the D5 chord played four times, each with an eighth note duration (half of a beat).

Beams

Smaller-valued notes are often grouped together using beams, with grouped notes typically spanning the length of one beat. It's noteworthy that rests are never beamed:

Dotted note

Additionally, notes and rests may be accompanied by a small dot, positioned just to the right of the rhythmic element. This dot extends the duration of the note or rest by one half.

Double-dotted note

The first dot elongates the note's duration by half, and the second dot further extends it by another quarter of the already elongated duration, equivalent to half of the preceding half.

Ties

Notes' durations can be extended through the use of ties. When tied, the following notes are sustained for the duration of the second note. It's important to note that rests are never tied together.

Grace-note before the beat

In musical notation, a grace note serves as an ornament, involving a swift note played just before another note. A grace note doesn't contribute to the bar's duration or rhythm display.

Grace-note on the beat

Similar to the grace note occurring just before the beat, one initiated precisely on the beat introduces a subtle delay in the onset of the subsequent beat.

Triplets

A triplet typically comprises three notes, collectively holding the duration of two notes of the same length when played. In the given example, notes are grouped in threes, where the duration of three of the triplet's eighth notes equals the duration of only one quarter note (not 8/3). Instead of dividing the quarter note by 2 to obtain eighth notes, it's divided by three. In standard music notation, these triplets usually have a '3' written underneath the group.

Swing Rhythm

In swing rhythm, the pulse is unevenly divided, with certain subdivisions (often eighth or sixteenth note subdivisions) alternating between long and short durations.

Repeats

The repeat sign in tab notation can be perplexing. When a pair of dots accompanies a double bar, it indicates that you must repeat the music either from the very beginning of the piece or from the previous repeat symbol, as follows:

In tab notation, it's crucial to follow the correct interpretation of repeat symbols. When you encounter repeat symbols with dots on the right side for the first time, disregard them. However, upon reaching a repeat symbol with dots on the left side, it signals that you should backtrack to the previous repeat symbol facing the opposite direction. In the absence of a previous symbol, return to the beginning of the piece. On subsequent encounters with the repeat symbol, ignore it unless it contains specific instructions like "3x" (indicating a repeat three times).

Alternate Endings

Sections often incorporate distinct endings after each repeat. For example, consider the illustration below, featuring a first and a second ending. Follow these steps: play until you encounter the first repeat symbol, then jump back to the previous repeat symbol (not shown in the picture). Continue playing until you reach the bracketed first ending, skip the measures beneath the bracket, immediately proceed to the second ending, and then resume playing.

Accented

An accented note calls for emphasis, a heightened attack on a specific note. Play this note louder than the others to highlight its significance.

Heavily accented

A heavily accented note demands maximum emphasis, an even more pronounced attack on a particular note. Play this note much louder than the others to create a distinctive impact.

Staccato

Staccato notation signals a very short note, regardless of the note's duration on the score. It directs the player to produce a brief and detached sound.

Popping

Popping is a technique commonly applied to bass guitars, involving a forceful plucking of one of the two highest strings using the right-hand index finger. This produces a sharp and percussive sound, adding a dynamic element to the music.

Slapping

Slapping is a technique predominantly employed on bass guitars. It entails the player hitting the strings with their right-hand thumb while rotating their wrist to generate a percussive sound. This technique adds rhythmic and percussive qualities to the bassline.

Tapping

Tapping involves striking a fret with your fingers without a preceding attack on the note, creating a distinct and often percussive sound.

Tremolo

Tremolo is characterized by rapid, short picking motions both up and down. In this technique, the pick exerts the same force on the string during both downward and upward movements. The hand remains as relaxed as possible to achieve high speed and fluidity.

Anacrusis

Anacrusis, also known as a pickup bar or upbeat, is a partial or incomplete bar appearing at the beginning or end of a tab. This bar will not be marked as erroneous, even if it is left incomplete, providing flexibility in the representation of the musical passage.

Jimi Hendrix
Purple Haze

Purple Haze

Track1: Fuzz Face Strat - Distortion Guitar

Jimi Hendrix

Purple Haze

Track2: Vocals - Electric Guitar (clean)

Jimi Hendrix

Jimi Hendrix
Voodoo Child

Voodoo Child Version1

Track 1 Jimi Hendrix - Distortion Guitar

Jimi Hendrix

Jimi Hendrix

All Along
the Watchtower

All Along the Watchtower

Track1 Guitar I - Overdriven Guitar

Jimi Hendrix

Tune down 1/2 step
①= E♭ ④= D♭
②= B♭ ⑤= A♭
③= G♭ ⑥= E♭

Moderate ♩ = 112

All Along the Watchtower

Track 2 Guitar II - Acoustic Guitar (steel)

Jimi Hendrix

Jimi Hendrix
Little Wing

Little Wing

Track 1 Strat - Electric Guitar (clean)
Jimi Hendrix

Tune down 1/2 step
① = E♭ ④ = D♭
② = B♭ ⑤ = A♭
③ = G♭ ⑥ = E♭

♩ = 68

72

Little Wing

Track 2 Glockenspiel - Electric Guitar (clean)
Jimi Hendrix

Jimi Hendrix
Hey Joe

Hey Joe

Track 1 Chords - Acoustic Guitar (steel)

Jimi Hendrix

Standard tuning

Moderate Rock ♩ = 84

Hey Joe

Track 2 Guitar 1 - Electric Guitar (jazz)

Jimi Hendrix

Standard tuning

Moderate Rock ♩ = 84

Count Off

Intro

Verse 1

Hey Joe

Track 3 Guitar 2 - Electric Guitar (jazz)

Jimi Hendrix

Standard tuning

Moderate Rock ♩ = 84

Interlude

Verse 3

Jimi Hendrix
Foxy Lady

Foxy Lady

Track 1 Jimi Rhythm Guitar - Distortion Guitar

Jimi Hendrix

END !!!

Foxy Lady
Track 2 Jimi Solo Guitar - Distortion Guitar
Jimi Hendrix

Jimi Hendrix
red house

Red house

Track 1 Jimi Hendrix - Overdriven Guitar

Jimi Hendrix

Verse 1

Verse 2

Main Solo

Verse 4 + Outro

Jimi Hendrix

Castles Made of Sand

Castles Made Of Sand

Track 1 Jimi Hendrix - Electric Guitar (clean)

Jimi Hendrix

Castles Made Of Sand

Track 2 Jimi Hendrix (Reverse Guitar) - Electric Guitar (jazz)

Jimi Hendrix

Jimi Hendrix
The Wind Cries Mary

The Wind Cries Mary

Track 1 Jimi (Guitar 1) - Electric Guitar (clean)

Jimi Hendrix

The Wind Cries Mary

Track 2 Jimi (Guitar Solo) - Electric Guitar (clean)

Jimi Hendrix

Jimi Hendrix
Manic Depression

Manic Depression

Track 2 Distortion Guitar

Jimi Hendrix

Jimi Hendrix
Crosstown Traffic

Crosstown Traffic

Track 1 Jimi (Lead) - Distortion Guitar

Jimi Hendrix

Outro

Crosstown Traffic

Track 2 Jimi (Rhythm) - Overdriven Guitar
Jimi Hendrix

Crosstown Traffic

Track 4 Jimi (Rhythm clean) - Electric Guitar (jazz)

Jimi Hendrix

Jimi Hendrix
Fire

Fire

Track 1 Jimi Hendrix - Overdriven Guitar 1

Jimi Hendrix

Fire

Track 2 Jimi Hendrix - Overdriven Guitar 2

Jimi Hendrix

Jimi Hendrix
Bold As Love

Bold As Love

Track 1 Strat - Electric Guitar (clean)

Jimi Hendrix

(song fades out)

Bold As Love

Track 2 Rhythm guitar - Electric Guitar (clean)
Jimi Hendrix

......Yeah!

(song fades out)

Bold As Love

Track 3 Overdub 1 - Electric Guitar (clean)

Jimi Hendrix

......Yeah!

(song fades out)

Bold As Love

Track 4 Overdub 2 - Electric Guitar (clean)

Jimi Hendrix

......Yeah!

(song fades out)

Bold As Love

Track 5 SFX Fuzz Face volume - Distortion Guitar

Jimi Hendrix

......Yeah!

(song fades out)

Jimi Hendrix
Stone Free

Stone Free

Track 1 Clean Guitar - Electric Guitar (clean)

jimi hendrix

verse 1

pre-chorus

chorus

204

drum solo

free time

guitar solo

Jimi Hendrix

Burning
Of the Midnight Lamp

Burning Of the Midnight Lamp

Track 1 Wah Wah Guitar - Electric Guitar (clean)

Jimi Hendrix

Standard tuning

♩ = 72

Burning Of the Midnight Lamp

Track 2 Guitar 2 - Electric Guitar (clean)

Jimi Hendrix

Jimi Hendrix

Spanish Castle Magic

Spanish Castle Magic

Track 1 Jimi Hendrix - Overdriven Guitar

Jimi Hendrix

Jimi Hendrix

If 6 Was 9

If 6 Was 9

Track 1 Hendrix - Rhythm - Electric Guitar (jazz)
Jimi Hendrix

Tune down 1/2 step
①= E♭ ④= D♭
②= B♭ ⑤= A♭
③= G♭ ⑥= E♭

♩ = 140

If 6 Was 9

Track 2 Hendrix - Solo - Electric Guitar (jazz)

Jimi Hendrix

Jimi Hendrix
Freedom

Freedom

Track 1 Overdriven Guitar

Jimi Hendrix

264

Unlock the full potential of Jimi Hendrix's iconic guitar tabs with the ultimate companion to this book. If you find yourself yearning for the exact location of a tab for any of the songs featured herein, look no further than our online store, where musical magic awaits. Visit us at

https://paidtabs.com/u/BlackBook,

and discover a treasure trove of musical mastery. Each song is meticulously crafted and available in PDF and GP formats that can be played on Guitar Pro. Immerse yourself in a more interactive and engaging experience as you explore the nuances of Hendrix's legendary tunes. Elevate your musical journey – dive into the soulful world of Jimi Hendrix with our premium tabs.

Thank You!

Thank you for choosing Jimi Hendrix Guitar Tab Book! We hope you've enjoyed playing and mastering the iconic songs of Jimi Hendrix. Your support means the world to us, and we're thrilled to be a part of your musical journey.

If you've found this book helpful and inspiring, we invite you to explore our other related books that cater to your passion for music. Whether you're a Christmas songs enthusiast or eager to dive into the world of guitar playing, our collection has something for every music lover.

Made in United States
North Haven, CT
25 February 2024

49167078R00154